HOW A JAIL CELL
SAVED CHRISTMAS

HOW A JAIL CELL SAVED CHRISTMAS

And What It Taught Me About
Finding Inner Peace

VERONICA R. de ALMEIDA

True Image
PUBLISHING

Published by: True Image Publishing
veronicardealmeida.com

Cover Design and Interior Book Design by
Francine Platt, Eden Graphics, Inc.
Source for cover photo: Pavel Kavalenkau

This book based on true events. It reflects the author's present
recollections of experiences over time. Some names and
characteristics have been changed, some events have been
compressed, and some dialogue has been recreated.

Paperback ISBN 979-8-89454-013-9
Ebook ISBN 979-8-89454-014-6
Audio book ISBN 979-8-89454-019-1

Library of Congress Number: 2024914135

Manufactured in the United States of America
First Edition
Second Printing

PRAISE FOR
HOW A JAIL CELL SAVED CHRISTMAS

"God is in the details of our lives. A must read any time of the year! *How a Jail Cell Saved Christmas* could more aptly be called 'how a jail cell saved *her*.' Veronica's beautiful story of how she found hope, peace and love to get through her own despair as she helps innocent men find hope in theirs shows us each that God is in the details of our lives. Sometimes we don't understand why we may be going through something till years later, but when we reflect and understand God's love and plan we will see the small everyday miracles that surround us. This story is an exemplar of that love and miracle!"

– TANYA HARRIS ROUNDY,
author of *Certainty: Walking Through Fire*

"A Christmas story to remember — a TRUE story of bitter betrayal, compassionate rescue, and finding FORGIVENESS."

– KATHY LEE PARKER,
Syndicated International Radio Talk Host

"A true and inspiring story. A story of disappointment and trying to survive, then a turn of events that took persistence and desire to help others. A great read!"

— **Paulette Ren**, author of *Stolen Moments*

"A remarkable book! *How a Jail Cell Saved Christmas* is a captivating read that had me hooked from the first page. The suspense, the lessons learned, and the steady pace make it impossible to put down. Based on a true story, it brings a unique and heartwarming twist to the Christmas narrative. Truly a remarkable book!"

— **Anais Cruz**, MS of Business Analytics

"A sad time can be a good time. The author's true story pulled me in and held me to the end. How does a tragic divorce and three young men in jail in a foreign country equate to a memorable and joyful Christmas? The story is told in this book. Merry Christmas."

— **Stan Cronin**,
author of *How to Date your Wife*

To my angel mother
who raised me to believe in the
true meaning of Christmas

Acknowledgments

I WOULD BE ungrateful if I didn't first and foremost acknowledge the fact that anything I do, who I am or will be, I owe to my Creator. I thank my Heavenly Father and the Lord Jesus Christ for giving me the chance to grow and for helping me share the lessons I've learned. They are the true authors of these stories.

I give heartfelt thanks to my sweetheart, confidant, and best friend, my dear husband Daniel. We have blended the finest family possible. I love you. Thank you for making me feel like I can do anything. Thank you for supporting my hobby of writing from the very beginning.

I am grateful for my parents, who gave me life. I'm particularly grateful for my angel mother, a woman of faith who has always exemplified with her compassion what it means to be a true disciple of Christ and who taught me the true meaning of Christmas.

Before sending the manuscript for editing. I felt inadequate and wanted some feedback. I thought of the most avid readers I knew and asked if they would be willing to review my manuscript. Millions of thanks go to—Cynthia Lippincott and Cheryl Boyle—for answering the call. They offered their time and talents without hesitation.

I send thanks to Val Johnson and Debbie Rasmussen for bringing the gift of editing to this book and for supporting my vision by offering words of encouragement. They were always willing to go the extra mile to improve my work. Without their patience and willingness to comment on ideas and suggest improvements, this book would never become a reality. Thank you!

This book would not have been written if it had not been for a dear friend, Nuria Martinez, my first editor; who suggested I publish the story. She said it needed to be told before I began to forget the details. Writing the book was something I had wanted to do. I just didn't know how to start. I will forever be grateful to her who motivated me to write my story in the first place. We all need friends like that.

Thank you!

Foreword

BY DR. NURIA MARTINEZ

I HAVE KNOWN Veronica Rodriguez de Almeida for over ten years. One of our first interactions was in the Dominican Republic. I had a youth handbell ensemble in Puerto Rico and the group had been invited to travel to the Dominican Republic to play at a musical event sponsored by our Church, The Church of Jesus Christ of Latter-day Saints. She wrote me an email offering to provide us with help in the way of food or rooms to stay. She let us know about logistics there and was very helpful throughout. I just mention this because it is in Veronica's nature to help and use her experience to ease the way of others if she can.

A year later, my husband and I were assigned to the Dominican Republic and guess who was waiting to help us find our way in the apartment? You guessed it!

Veronica was there to tell us where to turn on the water heater, where the light switches were, and who we could contact should an urgent matter arise. She brought us a welcome gift and made sure we knew how to get in touch with her in case we needed any other help. She later had us over for a meal. We enjoyed each other's company for the years we were there together.

When Veronica first told me the story of the bondsmen in El Salvador and how her interventions helped them return to the U.S., I was astounded! Here was this petite dark-haired woman who did a remarkable thing and few people, aside from those who participated in the incidents, know about it. I told her she should write her experience, not only because it was something that changed the lives of the men jailed, but so that others can see that one person can make a difference, one person with faith and gumption. It is remarkable that in the middle of one of her worst personal crisis, she would put her life aside momentarily to concentrate on the needs of others. Not only that, but Veronica also moved others into action: her mother, her uncle, and the judge. Who knows who else was inspired by her at that moment in time?

I read her first drafts and served as her first editor. Her finished book is a polished piece that puts in plain words what she went through and what those young men and their families suffered. She points out the hand of God moving and rousing others into actions that improved the circumstances of those young men. Hopefully, others will be inspired to act by reading her book. Maybe you will be inspired to do something good but difficult. If you are, I am sure Veronica would like to know because it might inspire you to follow Christ, too. And that is one of her aspirations, to bring others closer to Jesus Christ, to help them want to follow His example and become more like Him.

Note from the Author

MOST PEOPLE I KNOW have at least one obsession. Mine is Christmas. I love the higher quality time spent with friends and family. I look forward each year to the holiday season.

When I was growing up, my mother was obsessed with Christmas too, so much that our nativity scene took an area of about ten feet by six feet. Random people would come to our home to see it. She also prepared about 200 food baskets that she gave away. My mother did all that because of her love for Christ. She even named me after the Veronica who is known to be the woman who wiped the face of Christ as He carried the cross.

I presume that I get my love for Christ and Christmas from her.

For me, the Christmas season does not begin after the enormous Thanksgiving meal in November, but in September, shortly after the new school season begins. I learned to do that from the people in the Philippines, where Christmas formally begins on September 1st.

So, in September, I start purchasing gifts for the people on my list. I also get out all the boxes that have been stored for almost a year with a label that reads *Xmas* to prepare for that special December day. In the early days of Christianity, Christians used the letter *X* as a secret symbol to indicate to others their membership in the church. If you know the Greek meaning of *X—Chi—*the words *Xmas* and *Christmas* essentially mean the same thing.

After pulling out all the Xmas boxes, I look at what I have saved from years past and remove the dust from the decorations.

And that puts me in the mood for Christmas music. I'm probably the only person you know who starts listening to Christmas music in September. To me, there is nothing more sublime than the rendition of Handel's *Messiah* by the Tabernacle Choir. Does anyone else do that?

I love the twinkling lights, and festive decorated yards. I knew of a fellow in our neighborhood who decorated his home beautifully each year for all to see. He had thousands of lights to put up, so he started preparing for his display early in the fall. Perhaps some of us can relate!

I also start reading whatever new Christmas book has come out, watch all the classic Christmas shows. I go over talks, scriptures, podcasts, and anything else I can find that has been recorded about the life of Christ. I also get out my notebook marked *Xmas Stories.* My collection includes stories such as *The Christmas Orange, The Gift of the Magi, Christmas Eve 1881, The White Stocking, and Trouble at the Inn,* to name a few.

Do you have stories you like to revisit at Christmas? If so, you may want to add a new one to your collection: *How a Jail Cell Saved Christmas.*

Prologue

WE ALL, at some point in our lives, get our hearts broken. It's part of being human. It's so easy to be happy when things are going well, but what about those hard times? How do you ever pull yourself up from the depth of despair? This book will address how I found peace and joy at one of the darkest times in my life. Showing how to do that was the main reason I wrote this book.

I am a believer! Therefore, the perspective I share in this book reflects my religious upbringing and a bevy of personal insights I have gleaned from people who helped me cope at a time I found myself at the end of my rope. These friends were my ministering angels. They came to my aid and brought sunshine into my gloomy life.

Every chapter starts with a scripture dear to my heart. I also share inspirational quotes that were instrumental in helping me get through my agony. Most quotations come from the King James Version of the Bible. In a few cases, I quote other Bible translations. Where I have, I reference that translation.

This book is divided into two sections. Part One is *The Tale of Two Stories,* which consists of two incidents from my life. Part Two is *Lessons Learned,* which is self-explanatory. It is important to understand why we go through trials in life and what those hard times teach us. It's in those difficult moments when we grow most and become better people.

This book is meant to give hope to those souls experiencing pain so great that it may be preventing them from enjoying life. It is my desire to share what I discovered about how to find joy, peace, and hope amid the ashes of despair. It recounts experiences that took place mostly over a period during what had been my favorite time of the year. Each year, I had looked forward to celebrating Christmas.

Except not this year. I was not in the mood for parties or celebrations of any kind. My world as I knew it had collapsed, and I felt overwhelmed by darkness. I was at an extremely low point in my life. But I survived. Fortunately, I was thrust into a situation that not only saved my Christmas, but my sanity as well.

I have had some hesitation on what to write or not write. On one hand, I want to be genuine and real by sharing with you my insecurities and vulnerabilities with every lesson I've learned. Then, there is the other side of me that wants to keep things private to protect my personal life, my introvert side wants to keep things to myself. But I am also outspoken when advocating for a cause I care about and lately my cause and mission is to help you learn what took me years to know and understand. As I wrestle with what to do, I am not going to sugar coat it or pretend it didn't happen. I decided to be completely honest with you about who I am.

In some cases, I have changed names and altered personal information to protect the privacy of others, with a few, I was permitted to use their real names. The content comes from actual events. This story is taken out of my own life, and for that, I take full credit.

PART ONE

The Tale of Two Stories

And the peace of God, which passeth all understanding, shall keep your hearts and minds through Christ Jesus.

— PHILIPPIANS 4:7

A Daughter's Tears and Mine

*I*T WAS THAT TIME OF THE YEAR when I would normally be busy shopping for gifts and preparing for Christmas, but instead I went to see a therapist to make sure I was not going insane. The visit was prompted by a letter I found written by my twelve-year-old daughter.

> *School is now over, the bell of freedom rings. I'm overwhelmed with homework and a bunch of other things. Mama picks me up and Dad drops me off; I usually barely make it to class on time. It's only because you both want your "alone time."*

When I come home my daddy isn't back yet. I watch my mom go into her room to pray. I stand by the door and listen away; I can hear her voice crack as she cries. (You know, the worst thing you ever hear is the tears of your mother.) I think of flashbacks, of my childhood. I remember the things I would do. I had a perfect life; I went to church on Sundays with my mom, dad and sisters. I didn't care anyways. I thought life was just a game.

Then things started to fall into shame. Family members were starting to die. I could tell how upset my father was. Later, I noticed he had changed. He stopped going to church and became selfish and in love with himself. That's when my momma was never the same. She would cry a little every day. I knew something was wrong. I'm not that lame. I am not as stupid as you think. I could tell something was wrong before you could blink.

My mom and I are driving in the car to the store. She gets quiet. She has been doing that a lot lately. She turns around and asks me these hard questions. She gives me a choice I don't want. I want a family that doesn't break. I want my daddy to be the same. I can't stand it when my mom gives me that look, the look of confusion, and suffering too.

She is unhappy; she wants my dad to go. But she also wants what's best for all. She starts crying, I try to hold it in. It's hard to have a family that can last without breaking cause this world has changed, and it's rougher than old times. It is so sharp; it could even tear families. That is what it did to my family not too long ago. So now I am left with a decision of my own. Whether I want my happy mom, or an unhappy mom with dad. Either way it's a broken family. I wish sometimes that I could not have any. I wish that I could live on my own, away from this harsh world that holds broken families. It carries broken hearts that break every day. It carries broken dreams that ruin a person. That's kind of what happened to my dad. It also carries crimes and lots of sins. My only wish is to live away from this.

I want to be a hero, or maybe live on a humble farm. I want to be that pretty girl. I want to be that smart and have-talents girl. But every *day I get tossed and turned. This world I live in is starting to burn. But sometimes my parents act like I don't know, but I found out long ago. I am not as stupid as you think. I could tell something was wrong before you could blink. There is only one thing I don't understand. What went wrong and why is my life turning upside down?*

I stared at the words my daughter had written, as the broken pieces of my heart splinter even more.

Oh, no! I need to show this to Bruce.

He was sitting on the sofa, talking on his cell phone, and refused to make eye contact when I motioned to him. Finally, he got off the phone.

I handed him the letter. "I really don't want to be part of a broken family statistic. Can we go see a therapist? Please read this."

Bruce put his glasses on and started reading the letter while I waited patiently for him to finish.

A few moments later he took his glasses off and set them on the sofa's end table. Then he gave the letter back to me.

"She will be fine. "It will probably be good for her. It will make her strong and resilient."

"Resilient!" I shouted. "Isn't there a better way to be resilient than going through a pain like that?"

My eyes were swollen from crying, and I did something I had never done before except when praying. I got down on my knees, pressing my hands together, and pleaded, "Please reconsider what you are doing, Bruce! We have had a good, wonderful, happy family up till now."

His cold words cut right through me. "Don't you know, crying makes you look even uglier? And look at your alligator hands. Sometimes I feel as if I am in bed with my grandmother. I am sorry that I can't console you, Veronica, but I am not attracted to you, and I cannot be with a woman I don't love. Stop divorce busting!"

I stood grabbed his glasses, crushed them in my hands, and threw them on the floor. What I really wanted to do was strangle him for being so cruel to me.

His response left me tongue-tied, "You don't have me and you never will! Go to hell!" Then he stormed out of the house, slamming the door behind him.

Thou shalt love thy wife with all thy heart, and shalt cleave unto her and none else.

DOCTRINE AND COVENANTS 42:22

Broken Families

*T*HOSE OF US who have religion in our marriage know how we go over and beyond to protect the sanctity of the family. President Henry B. Eyring gave the final talk at the colloquium on marriage and family at the Vatican in Rome, Italy. Elder L. Tom Perry was in attendance and said, "President Eyring bore a powerful witness to the beauty of committed marriage and of our belief in the promised blessing of eternal families. ("Why Marriage and Family Matter—Everywhere in the world," *Ensign,* May 2015, 40-41)

In our home, we have "The Family: A Proclamation to the World" framed and hanging on a wall as a reminder and to refer to in case we get confused when the world around us tries to define what constitutes a family. This proclamation was given from the first presidency of The Church of Jesus Christ of Latter-day Saints in 1995. Here is an excerpt from it: "The Family is ordained of God. Marriage between man and woman is essential to His eternal plan. Children are entitled to birth within the bonds of matrimony, and to be reared by a father and a mother who honor marital vows with complete fidelity. Happiness in family life is most likely to be achieved when founded upon the teachings of the Lord Jesus Christ."

What I was experiencing in my marriage was opposite to what the proclamation says a family should look like. In fact, I discovered what hell looks like. I felt Satan's presence as if he were hysterically laughing at us, not just endorsing what was happening but urging us on. The feeling was dark. It became clear to me that I never would want to dwell in that ugly, dark space where Satan and his minions exist. I wanted nothing to do with the darkness I had been experiencing ever again!

There's a godlike quality in rejecting the idea of

divorce, but, unfortunately, divorce does happen. More and more often these days, it seems as if leaving your spouse for a new one is no different than exchanging an old car for a newer model.

I was incredibly confused by Bruce's rejection of me. Only a year before, he had written a love letter to me for Mother's Day.

I want to tell you on this special day that I love you and appreciate how hard you work. You are a loving mother, and your kids know that you love them. You are very supportive of me and my crazy work schedule. I know our life together hasn't gone as planned with my employment and our financial progress, but I hope you are not too disappointed. Hopefully things will go better this year and next until we can sell the business and try something new. Looking forward to more happy memories together.

So, I found a therapist. Dr. Alice Bell.

"I'm in shock," I told her. "How can someone change that fast? I don't know why I can't get this painful feeling out of me when I think of times when Bruce hurt me. It's hard to get motivated when your world collapses and there is not anything you can do about it. I just don't care about anything anymore."

She explained: "One of our frustrations with love is our inability to keep it. Like sand slipping between our fingers, the harder we grasp the faster it seems to fall through. It would be nice if love was as simple as baking a batch of cookies or building a treehouse for the backyard: a simple set of ingredients, a logical list of steps to take. But we all know the truth. Love cannot be manufactured. It cannot be bought or traded. It cannot be forced. It cannot be controlled. It cannot be plotted on a map or broken down into a checklist of to-do's."

"I understand. But what am I going to do with my negative thoughts, with the anger, with the unbearable hurt I feel?"

"We all will experience at one time or another those feelings: rejection, humiliation, desperation. Opening our hearts to another person, only to be rejected, is one of the most painful experiences in life. It hurts the most because in love we are most vulnerable. It's worse than physical pain because it shakes us at the core of our identity, our hopes, and our dreams. There is probably no topic that has captivated people throughout the centuries and in most every culture than the topic of love and break-up."

I sighed, "You can say that again"

"We put a man on the moon, broke the speed of sound, and mapped the human genome…"

"Wait a second, may I record this?"

Dr. Bell stopped, "Of course"

I clicked record on my phone. "okay I'm ready."

She continued, "But keeping love alive remains a complete mystery. Science has not been able to explain it. Mathematics cannot predict it. Poets still wrestle with adequate words to describe it. It may have been more than two millennia ago, but Plato's words have never sounded truer, every heart sings a song, incomplete.

"Love rushes us to the mountain top, and when lost, sends us back to the valley below. We cannot help but feel empty. We cannot help but feel worthless. We cannot help but feel hopeless—and you are entitled to those feelings—however, trust me on what I predict will happen: What you are experiencing now, one day will be a gift to you and your community. Your honesty and vulnerability are appreciated. Don't assume that everyone else is living an ideal life; you'd be shocked by how many people are experiencing the same as you. We are all looking for love. At any given moment, we may be far from it, but we never stop hoping the next opportunity is just over the horizon. We are all looking for true love, and one day you will find it."

Apparently, Bruce was still looking for true love. All I knew was that it was no longer me. Love after all is a choice, and he even said it himself, "I love you, but I am not in love with you."

I remember explaining to my therapist how I felt that Bruce was my cross.

"But what if the cross does not want to be carried?"

She opened my eyes when she said that.

Maybe it was time to let go.

During this time, I went to see a friend who is the only person in the world I knew had climbed the world's seven highest summits and sailed its seven seas. He is also very successful in business, and good-looking. It is hard to believe that someone as accomplished as he is suffered through a painful divorce. I thought he might have some good advice for me. This is a fellow who has my one hundred percent trust so I went to his office and shared my concerns.

"Veronica, we see people around us happily married and think to ourselves, Why not me? But don't go there. You are fine the way you are, and when you feel good about your situation and are happy with your life the way it is, miracles will happen. I had never been lonelier than in my marriage."

He was right. I needed to keep my chin up. We all learn to be resilient by experiencing a broken heart.

"Already too many {marriages} have broken hearts and broken homes because of broken covenants and broken promises. Society's increasing slide toward pleasure-seeking brings our so-called civilization comparatively closer to Sodom than to Eden." ("Be of Good Cheer," *Ensign,* Nov. 1982, 67–68).

Whenever people have asked, "Was there something you could have done?"

I usually answer, "Remember Princess Diana, beloved by millions of people around the world? If she could not keep her husband, Prince Charles, how on earth could I?"

And referring to my broken home, when people have asked why, I simply say, "Because people change, and you cannot trust a person who is not morally aligned, who lacks integrity and refuses to admit it."

The power of Satan is real, and if you are not doing the small and simple things to nourish your marriage, the way Elder Maxwell explained—especially, as in our case, if you have been married for time and all eternity—you are at a disadvantage when faced with Satan's efforts to tear your union apart. When Bruce and I stopped doing the basics, such as reading the scriptures together, attending the temple regularly, praying as a couple every day, even going to bed at the same time, we became an easy target.

At that point in my life, I found it comforting

to listen to or read inspirational words such as these from Elder Dieter F. Uchtdorf, an Apostle of The Church of Jesus Christ of Latter-day Sants. "Wherever you are, whatever your circumstances may be, you are not forgotten. No matter how dark your days may seem, no matter how insignificant you may feel, no matter how overshadowed you think you may be, your Heavenly Father has not forgotten you. In fact, He loves you with an infinite love" ("Forget Me Not," *Ensign,* Nov. 2011, 122-23).

It was clear to me that Bruce was gone. He didn't want to be with a forty-four-year-old woman when he could be with a woman our daughter's age. He was in the middle of what I now call a midlife crisis on steroids.

It all started when my brother-in-law passed away around Easter. Bruce took it hard and became very depressed. He decided to go on a trip to try to lift his spirits. There he met a woman, and after he got back he was never the same.

Nevertheless, I tried hard to hold on to my twenty-plus-year marriage just for our daughters. I didn't care about me. I only wanted the best outcome for our girls. I worried about our youngest sweet child, Mindy, who at the crucial age of twelve had written that heart-wrenching letter I shared earlier. I wanted, if possible, to take the pain away from her. This is what mothers do. But the truth is, I was helpless, and the only thing I did to cope with my emotions was to pretend that nothing serious was happening for as long as I could to buy time in hopes Bruce would come to his senses. I was willing to forgive him for the sake of my daughters and future grandchildren. I still couldn't seem to accept that his absence from my life and the family we had formed, would be permanent.

And whoso receiveth you, there I will be also, for I will go before your face. I will be on your right hand and on your left, and my Spirit shall be in your hearts, and mine angels round you, to bear you up.

DOCTRINE AND COVENANTS 84:88

Getting Served

I'M AMAZED when I think of all the people who have come to my aid at one time or another. In many cases, these people came out of nowhere to assist, console, support, sponsor, or sustain me in my trials each time I needed them the most. I believe these are ministering angels sent by heaven.

For instance, there was the time when my first born, Cristi, who had just turned one, was playing with a belt that had a hook on the end. The hook got caught in her eye, and as she struggled to pull the hook out, her eye started to come with it. When I saw what she was doing, all I could do was scream hysterically.

I screamed so loud that my upstairs neighbor

heard me. Nelson Bonilla quickly came to my aid and very carefully and calmly removed the hook from Cristi's eye. If not for his angelic assistance, my daughter could have lost her eye.

I also remember Carlos Merino, who would come to my house to shovel the snow or put the garbage out. He was not my next-door neighbor. Carlos lived on the other side of town, about a thirty-minute drive from me. He was an older fellow and a handyman who could fix anything. He was a good friend of my aunts from his youth and remembered me as a child. I could depend on him for all kinds of help.

Another time, a kind stranger took the time to help my lost toddler find her mother. I was inside a busy store and didn't know she had wandered away from me and was outside walking alone in the parking lot.

Then there was the time I had the nerve to knock on the door of my friend David Robinson, a doctor. My daughter was suffering from a rash that would not go away. He kindly took the time to examine her and diagnosed that the rash was caused by a type of flesh-eating bacteria. With his help, the disease was quickly controlled.

And how can I forget the wonderful priesthood blessings I've received from amazing priesthood leaders? Three bishops immediately come to mind: Bishop Bekker, Bishop Bouman, and Bishop Lowder, who wanted to help ease my pain from a pending divorce.

I can go on and on with story after story of so many people who have been angels to me, but I will focus on one story very close to my heart.

It was a cloudy and cold Saturday morning in October when my friend Maria and her mother Marilu came to see me. We were laughing and having a good time when we heard the familiar ding dong of the doorbell.

Mindy, my teenage daughter, went to answer the door and yelled: "Mom, it's for you!"

When I heard that, fear filled my heart.

Oh, please, please, please, let it not be,

I was in agony as I walked down the hall. My chest felt as though I was about to have a heart attack.

Mindy had left the door slightly ajar. I held my breath, and slowly pulled it open. I was afraid of who might be on the other side.

One month prior, my husband declared he wanted a divorce and decided to move out of the house. Because I had been afraid of being served with papers, I had not been answering the door if I was alone.

My fear materialized in front me as I exchanged awkward glances with a fellow I did not know who presented legal papers and a receipt for me to sign.

I saw for the first time in black and white my estranged husband's last name versus mine. I never had imagined we would someday get to this point of being matched against each other like opponents in a boxing ring.

———— ◆ ————

Bruce and I had been married for twenty-two wonderful years. We were very compatible when it came to doing humanitarian work, particularly during the Christmas season, when our home became Santa's little workshop.

People in our community knew we loved doing subs-for-Santa, and every year we found a family who needed help. Many of these friends and neighbors got on board and helped, too—so much that one year we played Santa for twelve families. We loved ringing the doorbell at people's homes, dropping off the presents carried in huge bags, and running back to the car as fast as we could.

Sometimes people knew who we were and thanked us for years. They may have just arrived from another country and carried with them only what they had on their backs, or they had been experiencing a hardship like a divorce, illness, or a job loss. Time and time again those families told us how much they appreciated what we did and how much they remembered that one Christmas. We loved helping in that way, and it became a family Christmas tradition.

But—what about this coming Christmas?

Bruce was always known for his big heart. He loved helping people, and I did too. We never argued or had any big disagreements. We were a solid match in the things that mattered most, one of which was our deep love for family and home. For decades, we were part of the same team, wanting the same things. We hid no secrets from one another, we would finish each other's sentences, we were devoted one to the other. Whenever our eyes would lock, we would blow kisses to each other.

At one time when we were first married, a professor asked Bruce, "What is your favorite hobby?"

"My wife!" He had quickly answered.

When we first got married, he wrote in his journal,

I want to always be able to say I love Veronica more today than I did yesterday. I worry that in the future I might forget my determination to make our marriage a success and the best thing in life. I hope that we are always the best of friends before anything else. I want to make the commitment now that I will show her my appreciation and my love for her by the little things I can do for her, like gifts and love notes and things like that. I really and honestly think we're going to be the happiest couple around. It's great to be in love. It's hard if not impossible to describe the attraction I feel toward Veronica. I want so much to love her and make her happy and feel the love I have for her. I don't know the trials the future holds in store for us, but if I can always remember the love I feel for her, then I believe I could give my life for her were it necessary.

Bruce had eyes only for me because for many years I was young and beautiful. But slowly I aged, and some men going through a midlife crisis have a problem seeing themselves with an older woman; perhaps it forces them to see that they are getting old, too. All was fine as long as I looked young, but eventually the morning came when he told me he was no longer in love with me. Not long afterward, the man with the divorce papers came to my door.

I stared at those papers. I was left speechless, numb, and in shock. Our beautiful love story had ended. Tears streamed down my face as I carried the papers back into the kitchen where my friends were, and after a moment of silence I told them the truth; there was no more pretending that we were a perfect family.

I cleared my throat, "This is it. It's over!"

We threw our arms around each other, forming a circle in a group hug. I don't remember what they told me, but Marilu, a woman in her eighties with great wisdom, spoke to me in a way that made me feel better.

Looking back, I think Marilu and her daughter Maria were heaven-sent. Maria a.k.a. Chachis, is a friend I have known since we were in college and someone I love like my own sister. When she and her mother first came to my house that day, I wondered what on earth made them stop by. They never had come over spontaneously before. In the past when they came, it was for dinner, or a party, or some other event. But here they were when I needed them most. The fact that my best friends had come to visit me precisely at that moment was a tender mercy. That day, I felt the love of my Heavenly Father.

"I testify of angels, both the heavenly and the mortal kind. In doing so I am testifying that God never leaves us alone, never leaves us unaided in the challenges that we face. And always there are those angels who come and go all around us, seen and unseen, known and unknown, mortal and immortal" ("The Ministry of Angels," *Liahona,* Nov. 2008, 30-31).

Divorce in today's society is no longer shocking, but it is still a surprise when two people who are married, no matter what their religion, have experienced a long and seemingly happy marriage only to see their union dissolve. In my church, The Church of Jesus Christ of Latter-day Saints, we make some very distinct and serious covenants when we get married in the temple for time and eternity. Those covenants are much like what Adam and Eve made, and they are everlasting. They are not to be taken lightly because serious consequences follow if we don't preserve our part of the covenant relationship. This is what makes a temple marriage annulment even more tragic. Conversely, when we do keep those sacred covenants, we are eligible to obtain the promise from God of exaltation in His presence forever.

Our youngest was in sixth grade at the time, and as hard as we had been trying to pretend we were a happy couple, she could sense the tension.

One Sunday that fall when the weather started to get colder, we got up to attend church the same way we had countless times before. It was a snowy day and Bruce refused to join us. He said he would rather go skiing.

"Furthermore," he had said, "On a good day, I would rather go hiking."

Keeping the Sabbath day holy is what we do as a family. We follow scripture and dedicate this one day to the Lord, foregoing our own pleasure. There is no written law stating what to do or not to do on the Sabbath; it is an individual thing. But for our family, Sunday had always been the day we went to church together even on vacation. The rest of the day, we visited family members or someone who was ill.

For me it was also a day for a "siesta." Yes, I loved my Sunday's nap. We didn't go to work, shopping, the movies, concerts, sport events, or parties. In fact, we didn't do anything that we normally did on any other day.

Not going to church with us signaled the beginning of Bruce's change of heart. As his personality changed, it was like I didn't know who he was anymore. Leaves were falling and the weather outside was changing the same way my marriage had become less warm and more frigid. I could tell something was wrong, but I couldn't put my finger on it.

...They had been taught by their mothers, that if they did not doubt, God would deliver them. And they rehearsed unto me the words of their mothers, saying: We do not doubt our mothers knew it.

– ALMA 56:47-48

4

A Mother's Plea

*I*T WAS ONE OF THOSE dreaded Monday mornings right after I was served with the divorce papers. It was almost noon; I was feeling depressed, and I hadn't even gotten out of bed when the phone rang.

The caller ID showed a number I didn't recognize. At first, I didn't want to answer the phone because I figured it was probably a robocall. However, a prompting encouraged me to take the call.

"Hello, Veronica speaking."

"Hi, Veronica. Are you the Honorary Consul of El Salvador?"

"Yes," I had no idea who was calling me, but I could tell from her voice the woman was anxious and agitated.

"J. P. gave me your phone number. He told me that you are well connected in El Salvador and would probably know what to do. I need help for my son Eddy. He is in jail with a co-worker and their boss. I know he is innocent of whatever he is being accused of doing. He's a good boy."

"May I ask what happened?"

"I don't know exactly, other than my son and the two others plus three policemen were arrested at the San Salvador airport last Saturday. They were attempting to leave the country with a man who needed to come back to the U.S. My son's boss owns a bail bond company in Las Vegas, and they were not aware they were doing anything wrong. Eddy does not know Spanish. He doesn't understand what they are saying…"

"You mean to tell me that your son does not know what he has been arrested for?"

"That is right!"

I could only imagine how insane it would be if I had a child thrown into jail in a foreign country without understanding the language. I placed myself in her shoes and told her, "Let me call some people to find out more about this case. I will call you back."

My family's favorite place on the planet is El Salvador. Despite all the bad press, our country is our heaven on earth. In English, *El Salvador* means, "The Savior"

I am from there, so naturally my family in the United States started going there to visit from the time my girls were babies. That is where they learned Spanish.

Year after year we went back to my homeland. I could offer my family a trip anywhere in the world, but they would still choose El Salvador first. It has held a special place in our hearts.

In 2001, a massive earthquake followed by another one only one month later shook the town where I was born. All the destruction kept me awake at night thinking of all those people who had lost everything. I called my family and friends I knew in government to ask if there was anything I could do, and that is when I was appointed the Honorary Consul of El Salvador in the state of Utah.

In that role, I took many calls from Salvadorans

who feared deportation and didn't know what to do. Some were concerned about what to do with their children who were U.S. citizens. Others had worse problems; they found themselves in jail because they had been using fake Social Security numbers, which is a serious felony.

However, this time, the call did not come from a Salvadoran national but from an American woman, who feared for her son. As a mother myself, I could feel her pain.

I have made up many excuses to go to El Salvador, but this time it was urgent. My throat was dry and itchy, and my head was pounding as if I was getting a cold.

I had been crying nonstop for two days, and my eyes were red and swollen. In fact, my whole body felt like a train had run over it. I was feeling sick to my stomach, unable to eat or sleep, and I had lost weight. Nevertheless, I felt compelled to do something, anything to help her son.

There were also my gut feelings. Some call it intuition. Too often we don't pay attention to those promptings, but they are incredibly important.

Even the simplest nudges can have profound effects on the choices we make. I learned the hard way that if I don't act when those feelings come, I regret it later. I was smart enough to pay attention this time.

Ask, and it shall be given you; seek, and ye shall find; knock, and it shall be opened unto you.

– MATTHEW 7:7

Asking for Help

*Y*OU OFTEN HEAR PEOPLE SAY, "It's not what you know but who you know." I've often found that to be true.

I was aware of a situation a year earlier in which a girl from Bolivia tried to enter El Salvador without a visa. Let's call her Sofia. She was coming from Utah with the group "Help International" to do humanitarian work. All were U.S. citizens except for her. The airline should have detected that, but it was overlooked, and Sofia got on board. One by one all her friends purchased the required tourist visa as they came into the country, except for her. Sofia had a Bolivian passport, and that required a special visa to enter El Salvador.

She was denied entry.

Requirements change constantly, and that's one reason why the airlines are usually very careful about checking transit documents. You should always check to see if you need a visa for the country you are traveling to, before you purchase a ticket.

I was in Salt Lake City at a book club meeting with my friends when I got the call about Sofia. It was getting late in the evening, and poor Sofia was told she would spend the night at the airport. The airline planned to send her back to Los Angeles early the next morning.

I spoke with El Salvador's consul general in Los Angeles so he would be expecting her. He said he would visit with her as soon as she arrived at his office. In the meantime, I decided to look for someone in El Salvador who had the authority to allow Sofia into the country.

Normally, I would have talked to Francisco Flores, the president of El Salvador at the time. He was a classmate, friend, and cousin, but he was out of town. Instead, I spoke with everybody I could think of; airport security representatives, administrators for the airline, government ministers and vice ministers.

Eventually I contacted the secretary of the vice president, Liliana Hernandez, who was a member of the Church of Jesus Christ of Latter-day Saints like me. We knew each other well. Sister Hernandez understood the problem, and she knew the girl had come to do humanitarian work with the "Help International" group. She told me she would ask the vice-president if she could sign a document on his behalf to arrange for Sofia to be admitted into El Salvador without a visa.

In the early hours the next morning before Sofia needed to board the plane back to Los Angeles, Liliana called me to let me know the problem had been resolved. Sofia was granted a special visa waiver to get her paperwork done in San Salvador rather than going back to Los Angeles just to turn around.

She was told to go immediately to the consulate office nearest the airport, where she could get her documentation in order. Thanks to my dear friend, Liliana Hernandez, Sophia, a Bolivian national, could clear customs without a regular visa to start doing her humanitarian work with the rest of the group. What a miracle!

Remembering the experience, I thought perhaps I could help the young men the same way. Of course, it's one thing to obtain a visa and another to be freed from jail.

I started by calling my family in El Salvador and asking them to find out what happened at the airport. They immediately jumped in to help. My mother talked to everyone she knew about the bondsmen; they were known locally in El Salvador as the bondsmen because they worked for a bail-bond company.

We confirmed that indeed the American young men were in serious trouble.

My mother reported, "I couldn't believe they thought they could take someone back to the U.S. without a passport. The newspapers are spreading rumors of them being charged with kidnapping, but they don't look like the type. I think they are innocent."

My sister called the president of El Salvador. She honestly thought the president of the country could do something to help get the young men out of jail, but he explained that in cases like this it's up to the judge and their attorney. The only thing he said was, "I hope they've got a good lawyer!"

"Finally, brethren, whatsoever things are true, whatsoever things are honest, whatsoever things are just, whatsoever things are pure, whatsoever things are lovely, whatsoever things are of good report; if there be any virtue, and if there be any praise, think on these things. Those things, which ye have both learn, and received, and heard, and seen in me, do: and the God of peace shall be with you."

PHILIPPIANS 4:8–9

The Cell

WHEN I LEARNED that this case would be in the hands of a judge and a lawyer, I knew I needed to find out who they were. You'd think that the president of a country could get someone out of jail, but I knew he didn't bend rules.

He told my sister, "In my administration the power to release prisoners relies strictly on the judicial system, not the executive."

This was bad news for the young men. Apparently, they were charged with not only pretending to be FBI agents but also with kidnapping. They were looking at the very real possibility of spending years in a Salvadoran prison.

I felt I had to go to El Salvador. I needed to talk

face to face with the young men being detained, the people at the U.S. embassy, the newspaper reporters who were spreading rumors, their lawyer, and even the judge, if possible. I arranged for my daughter Mindy to be taken care of at home while I booked the next flight to El Salvador.

I love going to El Salvador whenever possible. Any excuse will do. My journal has the following entry for Thanksgiving 2012:

I am grateful for this beautiful world and for the blessing of living abroad, visiting so many different places in every corner of the world. It's no secret that I love to travel. One year, I went around the world five times, but one place so close to my heart is my place of birth. I miss waking up to the sound of crashing waves, the song of birds or roosters crowing. I love watching the beautiful sunsets and hundreds of stars at night. I was born in El Salvador, a country that bears the Savior's name, and for that, I am grateful.

It felt good to be home again. The first thing I did when I arrived was to find out where the bondsmen were being held. When I went to visit them in jail, all three were sitting on the floor in a small room with no light except for a small opening at the top of the ceiling. There were no beds or other furniture in the room. The hard floor was dirty and probably infested with cockroaches. That dark, filthy room was more of a dungeon than a jail cell.

When they saw me, they all stood. Their anguished faces haunted me for days. They told me that U.S. embassy officials had visited them and said that they would probably end up in a high-security prison for at least six years. In El Salvador that would be worse than the City jail. It is horrendous!

A prison in some places around the world could be consider a resort compared to a one in El Salvador.

I remember going to see a fellow in California who had been charged with smuggling drugs in his sailboat. He had access to all kinds of recreational activities, great food, and even entertainment. Not in El Salvador. You don't ever want to be locked up there with hard-core criminals.

I called Sydney, Eddy's mother. She is the woman in the U.S. who had initially contacted me. I wanted to report on what I had learned and to get more information about her son. She assured me that her son always did the right thing. He had just returned from serving a mission for The Church of Jesus Christ of Latter-day Saints and was temple worthy.

At age eighteen, some young men and women of The Church of Jesus Christ of Latter-day Saints leave the comfort of their homes, their family, and their friends to serve God full time for eighteen months to two years. To become a missionary, you need to show that your life reflects a high standard of morality and integrity and that you are willing to leave everything behind for the duration of your mission. I know they need to show that they are honest in all their dealings and that they are worthy to hold a temple recommend. Those who do serve, have my deepest respect.

Those who enter the mission field are often verbally and even physically attacked. Some have to learn a difficult new language in extremely harsh living conditions. But they go anyway because they are committed disciples of Jesus Christ and want to serve Him the same way the Apostles in the Bible did. Their purpose in going is simply to bring people closer to Christ. They share the messages found in the scriptures.

I have known many of these missionaries personally. Some have been members of my own family. I am not implying that they are perfect, but I believe them to be trustworthy. And I believed that Eddy and friends were telling the truth. I couldn't imagine these young men remaining in the predicament they were in. So, after leaving them, I spoke with their lawyer over the phone.

He explained, "There was a misunderstanding. They were not pretending to be FBI agents, and they were not kidnapping anyone."

But the newspapers were reporting otherwise. Something here didn't make sense.

…I was in prison, and ye came unto me.

MATTHEW 25:36

7

The Story Makes the News

*M*Y PARENTS had been in the broadcasting business for decades, so I called the news director at our own YSKL radio station. He didn't have to look too hard because the story was all over the news. These Americans were detained in El Salvador for supposedly committing serious crimes. I told him that after visiting with the American bondsmen, I felt compelled to believe these young men were innocent.

I asked the young men if they had received any assistance from the embassy.

Eddy told me, "No, other than a fellow who seemed very sarcastic; he did not believe our story. He was no help at all."

So, the American embassy was my next stop.

I felt I had to talk to the staff in person in hopes they would believe me.

While I was waiting to see the consul general, I noticed a copy of the local newspaper next to my chair. It had unflattering photos of the young men on the front cover.

There is no way they will get a fair trial if the papers are spreading awful rumors of their character.

The story in *La Prensa Grafica* read:

San Salvador, El Salvador—Salvadoran police have arrested three U.S. bail bondsmen at the airport in San Salvador, alleging that the Americans posed as FBI agents in an attempt to abduct a Salvadoran citizen, Salvadoran authorities confirmed Sunday.

The three men were arrested Saturday as they attempted to leave the country with a Salvadoran national who was accused of raping a minor in Las Vegas and were seeking to turn him over to authorities in Nevada.

The U.S. Embassy in San Salvador confirmed the arrests and said the Americans were not employed by the FBI or any other government agency, according to a news release from Salvadoran federal police. An embassy official would not provide more information about the detainees.

Another newspaper, *Prensa Latina,* contained the headline "U. S. Agents Violate Salvadoran Sovereignty." The story that followed was alarming:

San Salvador—Diverse Salvadoran organizations considered Tuesday that the attempt by three U.S. agents to kidnap a Salvadoran citizen and take [him] to the U.S. is a severe violation of Salvadoran sovereignty.

"This is a serious offense to the Salvadoran nation's sovereign character," said Mr. Amaya of the Foundation for Study and Application law.

Last week, three U.S. agents were arrested in the international airport of Comalapa, El Salvador, when they tried to illegally remove a Salvadoran citizen, who allegedly committed a sexual violation in the U.S. state of Nevada.

The U.S. agents, considered bounty hunters by the Salvadoran press, are employed by the private enterprise, Dirty Deeds Bail Bonds.

The U.S. individuals claimed to be members of the U.S. FBI. The U.S. Embassy in El Salvador denied this.

An anonymous source from the U. S. Embassy stated that the U.S. agents did not coordinate their actions with the Embassy.

Salvadoran deputy Oscar Fernandez asked for the case to be thoroughly investigated, and the full weight of the law applied to those responsible. "They didn't do it by the book and that's what they get."

When I was ushered in to see the consul general, I shared my concerns and belief that the young men were innocent. He said in a sarcastic tone, "Our hands are tied. They committed serious crimes, punishable by law in this country, and they need to pay for them."

I admit to raising my voice a little. "I thought in your country a person is considered innocent until proven guilty!"

I was shocked at his coldness and indifference. At that point I knew the embassy was no help. I stormed out of the building. They were not going to change their minds.

Isn't it ironic that no one was concerned about the real felon who raped a minor in Las Vegas and was hiding in El Salvador?

Next I went to speak to the people at "*La Prensa Grafica*" to file a formal complaint against the newspaper. The owners are friends of our family.

So, I took the liberty of going directly to see them in person. I couldn't believe that they would print unsubstantiated rumors and outright lies just to sell copies of the paper.

All that negative press about the American bondsmen wasn't helping the young men. When people read a story in a reputable paper they take it at face value, thinking the reporters have done their homework and are telling only the truth. But in this case, I knew better. I knew the paper was exaggerating. Since the subjects of their stories were Americans, the staff knew they could gain attention by pandering to an anti-American bias and painting the three young men as criminals.

I told the news director how disappointed I was at what they were doing with their "fake news" and demanded equal space in the paper when the young men were found innocent. He said that he honestly thought the newspaper was telling the truth.

I asked him, "How do the reporters know what is true?"

"They base their reporting on facts."

That is when I knew those young men were doomed. No one believed them except for a few good people like my sister, my uncle, and my mother. Still, I was committed to continue the fight.

If you always choose to do what is right, it doesn't matter what the outcome is. You succeed simply because you tried to do your best. That is what matters. And there is no better feeling than knowing you did the right thing. Even when no one believed me, I felt I had to say something to the people who were taking advantage of the situation.

*And I was led by the Spirit, not knowing
beforehand the things which I should do.*

– 1 Nephi 4:6

What to Do?

*U*NSURE WHAT TO DO NEXT, I counseled with some friends. I described what had happened to the young men and confided that I believed them to be innocent. No one believed me! Each person I talked to advised me to stay out of the mess and not get involved, warning me that I could end up in jail as an accomplice.

Notwithstanding, I felt compelled to do something. I believed the bondsmen, even if no one else did—except for my uncle, my sister, and my mother. If it weren't for their support, I wouldn't have had the courage to continue. In fact, each played an important part in what followed.

My uncle Charlie knew where to get information

and how to get around El Salvador. He was the one who found the jail the American bondsmen were in. He became my driver and took me whenever and wherever I needed to go. I would have been lost in the country if it had not been for him. He collected every story he saw in the paper and gave them to me to read.

My sweet sister Liz couldn't possibly imagine that those young men were criminals. She was the one with all the connections. She had lived in El Salvador for years and had married into a very respected family. She and her husband were people of influence and were especially well known for their integrity. Their position on the innocence of the Americans helped sway the opinion of several important people.

And of course, there was *Yaya,* my angel mother who had a big heart and much-needed resources. When it was time to post bail for the three young men, she came through, taking thirty thousand dollars (30,000) from her savings.

The four of us had a few things in common. For starters, we were all aware of the high ethics of the members who belong to The Church of Jesus Christ of Latter-day Saints and hold a temple recommend. Next, we had all traveled abroad and knew how easy it is to break a law you don't know or understand. And finally, we were all parents and could empathize with Eddy's mother, thinking how sad it would be to have a child in jail in a foreign land, especially knowing that they are innocent.

As we counseled together—and with the Lord—about what to do, one thing became clear. I had to talk to the most important person involved in the case, the judge.

...And that such as will administer the law in equity and justice should be sought for and upheld by the voice of the people...

— Doctrine and Covenants 134: 3

The Judge and I

I NEEDED TO TELL THE TRUTH—the whole truth, and nothing but the truth—to the judge. I arrived early in the morning at the courthouse to make sure I could get in. It was close to the airport, about an hour away from where I was staying at my parent's home.

I showed the woman at the front desk my honorary consul credential and said, "May I speak to the judge, please?"

The secretary looked puzzled. Perhaps she thought I was someone important.

She told me that she would make the necessary arrangements for me. "I will let you know as soon as the judge has a break."

It turned out that the judge was a woman.

We're in luck. She might feel some compassion for the plight of a mother.

As I stepped inside her chambers, I remembered watching TV shows where people say: "Your Honor," which in Spanish is *Su Señoria*. So that is exactly what I did.

I spoke to her in Spanish.

"Your Honor, I'm here to talk about the American bondsmen. I wasn't sent by anyone. I came on my own. I am not a lawyer or getting paid to do this, but I am a mother, and as a mother I would hate to see my child jailed when I know he did nothing wrong intentionally. I can assure you that those young men are innocent. They are very naïve and find themselves in this precarious situation because they didn't know what they were doing."

The judge looked at me and nodded as if she approved.

I pressed further, "They need to be on house arrest until they are sentenced."

She furrowed her brows, "But doing that is risking the chance that they will escape."

"No, they won't" I said firmly. "You can be completely at ease that they will comply with all that is demanded of them until their sentencing. I will make sure of that. You have my word."

I don't know how I got the nerve to say what I did, but I remembered going to a seminar where the instructor said, "At times you are going to be asked to do hard things, and your mind will tell you that you can't because you feel insecure or inadequate or incapable, but you need to stop that thinking and start pretending you are on a movie set and playing a part."

She had said loudly, "All you need to do is to play the role with confidence and act your part. In life, confidence is the only thing you need to fake."

The break was over. The judge's secretary came in to let her know that she needed to get back to the courtroom, but I felt I had connected with her. I sensed that I had touched her heart as a mother and that she was probably going to support my plea, thanks to my title as the honorary consul of El Salvador to Utah.

Every letter I received as honorary consul had

Honorable written before my name. I loved that. Of any titles I have received, *Honorable* is my favorite.

At the next hearing, the judge allowed the three young men, Eddy, Richard, and Thomas to be on house arrest.

She stretcheth out her hand to the poor;
yea, she reacheth forth her hands to the needy.

— PROVERBS 31:20

10

The Need for Cash

A HOUSE ARREST is much better than jail. In a cell, you are locked up twenty-four-seven in a small room. To get out, you need a trial to determine if you will be set free.

On house arrest, you are free to roam around your home as if you were in quarantine. Lucky for the bondsmen, they found a home for rent next to the courthouse. They could stay inside that home while the trial was pending. Getting out of that jail was a huge improvement in their situation.

However, there were a few conditions for the house arrest. They were going to be watched very carefully. Every morning they all needed to go to the courthouse to sign in, but other than that, they would be free to roam not only inside the home but also they could go out of the home if they did not go beyond the limits of the town.

To enjoy that kind of freedom, limited as it was, they each needed to come up with ten thousand dollars (10,000); times three, that total would be thirty- thousand dollars (30,000) for bail money. The need for cash was urgent.

Fortunately, my mother was able to provide the funds—which was somewhat miraculous because my mother never had that amount of money in cash. If for some reason she happened to have any on hand, she usually had it committed to pay a debt or invested in some business venture. I had never known my mother to have that much money saved. But for some reason she did this time. I went with her to the bank; the money was in a certificate of deposit and we learned that she could take the money out without having to pay a penalty. The woman who helped us waived the fees.

We immediately took the check to the courthouse, as the bail had to be paid that day or the bondsmen would be sent to prison. When we delivered the check, just imagine our faces showing panic when we were told that there was a mistake. It was made to the wrong institution. We would have to get a new check.

So, we raced back to the bank, arriving five minutes before it closed. The cashier we had worked with earlier was still inside.

We explained our problem and stressed how important it was that a new cashier's check be made out that same day. The suspense was intense because every second counted.

With a new corrected check, we took off running, with the intent on getting it turned in before the courthouse closed at 5:00 p.m. We arrived at 4:55 p.m.

Wherefore, by their fruits ye shall know them.

— 3 Nephi 14: 20

11

The Untold Story

ON October 31, I went to the courthouse to ask permission to take the bondsmen to San Salvador to do some shopping. I explained to the judge, "They don't have anything in that house, and they need to buy pillows and blankets and other necessities. This little town doesn't sell those kinds of things."

The judge agreed.

So, the next day I came to take the young men to the big city. Our first stop was at a mall to eat at a restaurant. As we are about to order, they all got up at once to use the restroom. I waited for what I thought was an eternity for them to come back. Maybe escaping had not even crossed their minds, but I started to get very nervous. I began to wonder if I had made a mistake taking them out.

What if they leave?

I had given my word this would not happen, and I imagined my picture plastered on the front page of the newspapers being taken into custody. I closed my eyes to say a prayer, and then as I opened my eyes I saw the young men seating themselves at our table. I felt bad that I had thought they might not come back.

The next day, November 2nd, was a holiday known as *Dia de los Muertos.* It is a day the courthouse is closed. For Eddy, Richard, and Thomas, it meant that they didn't have to sign in. I had the brilliant idea to take them to my family's beach house.

My uncle took us there, and for just one day, those boys played like little kids. They acted as if nothing was wrong. Finding themselves in a different place, surrounded by people who cared about them for a change, they seemed relaxed and truly carefree despite their circumstances.

The next day when we took them back to town, the police stopped us. I knew we were probably speeding. I was super nervous because I had not asked permission to take them out of town overnight. They were supposed to come back to their home each night, and they were never supposed to leave town. But the police didn't even ask us about the Americans sitting in the backseat of the car. The officer just asked us to slow down.

Whew!

When we finally returned the young men to their house, I felt a sense of relief.

Looking back, I now realized how risky it was for me to take the young men out of town. I could have ended up in jail too and jeopardize their case. My reasoning for taking them to the beach house was because I knew they were innocent. I felt they needed a break. In retrospect, If I had to do it again, I would not have done it.

It was time for me to return home. I had done all I could do for them so, I left my mother and sister in charge. Every single day for the next two months one of them would call to let me know of any news.

Every day, the young men had to go to the courthouse to sign in. They had to endure one court appearance after another, but never learning their fate.

While they waited for a decision, they spent some time doing service in the community. They went to some of the schools and taught English to the students; they also coached them on how to play basketball. Many of the schoolgirls had crushes on them. They created a good name for themselves, and people in town came to view them as "nice boys." Of course, that helped them greatly in their case.

And ye shall know the truth,
and the truth shall make you free.

– JOHN 8:32

12

Finding My Freedom

WHEN I ARRIVED back home in Utah, I discovered a secret. During the time I was away, I had forgotten about my pending divorce. I was too busy preparing for Thanksgiving to give my absent husband much thought.

One day as I was thinking about what I was thankful for, all of a sudden it hit me—I was free. Unlike those young men in El Salvador, I could come and go and do anything I wanted. I was reminded how precious my freedom was.

True, I was experiencing a hard time in my life, but at least I was free. I could make choices and do what pleased me, not somebody else. I liked the idea of being independent. My involvement in that case had cured me of feeling sorry for myself and taught me to accept things as they were. The phrase "Bad things happen to good people" came into my mind. I was not the exception.

By Thanksgiving, news about my divorce had spread widely. My friends and family were shocked. They couldn't believe that Bruce—wise, dependable, industrious, honest, deeply religious Bruce— had changed so dramatically and was determined to end our marriage.

My neighbor asked, "Has Bruce seen a doctor lately for a check-up?"

"Do you think he might have a brain tumor?" My mother thought it could be a possibility.

"Is there anything you could have done?" a friend dared asked me.

I assured this person, "I gave all I had to give but it wasn't enough."

I had spent so much time and energy in trying to free those young men in El Salvador that I had put my pending divorce completely out of my mind. It was now time to get back to reality.

My reality!

Bruce had changed so much that I didn't even know who he was anymore. I was hoping for a miracle, for him to come back to his old self.

I waited and waited . . .

Marriage...there is nothing else quite like it. It's the best of times, the most trying of times, the funniest of times, the hardest of times, and the very best thing you will ever do in this life if you choose a companion that's committed to staying in the marriage. Your best choice will be someone devoted to staying on the straight and narrow path that leads to eternity with you and who in moments when either of you start wandering off—will call the other out quickly to ensure that you both stay on a path you can continue walking together forever.

Back in my dating days as a single young woman I was under the impression that it was important to marry someone who was compatible in as many areas of life as possible. Someone with the same religious, educational and socio economic background. The more similarities, the better your chances. However, what I discovered is that even though those things are important, a happy marriage is not guaranteed. Many non-religious people and others from different educational or socio-economic backgrounds have great marriages. What counts in the end is marrying someone with integrity and commitment to the marriage. Simple as that!

Love is patient, love is kind. It does not envy, it does not boast, it is not proud. It does not dishonor others, it is not self-seeking, it is not easily angered, and it keeps no record of wrongs.

1 CORINTHIANS 13:4–5, NEW INTERNATIONAL VERSION

13

Love Is Patient

I WANTED SO MUCH to keep the tension between Bruce and me from tarnishing Mindy's good childhood memories, but it was too late. The divorce was grinding towards the inevitable. Slowly I realized how day by day, actually if I were honest, for years, Bruce and I were becoming more like roommates than a married couple.

I recalled one night, months earlier waking up with pain so severe I thought I was going to die. Bruce was still sleeping, so, not wanting to wake him, I got up and drove myself to the emergency room in the middle of the night. The next thing I knew, doctors were telling me they had to take out my gallbladder. As I waited in the operating room, I started to cry.

It doesn't get any lonelier than this!

Right before I had my gallbladder removed I was in denial, trying hard to save my marriage. Bruce had not expressed his decision to moved out yet for the sake of our oldest daughter, who was planning her wedding. At the same time, I was trying to keep things the way they were before Bruce changed in hopes that he might reconsider. I struggled for months to keep up appearances.

"Veronica," he would say, "please stop divorce busting. Don't you get it? Insanity is doing the same thing again and again hoping for a different result."

But I refused to give up.

Later that April, I was opening the mail when I came across a letter from a bank. At first I thought it was a solicitation because it was from a bank I didn't recognize. But before throwing it away, I decided to open it.

The letter showed that a substantial amount of money had been transferred from a bank account in Bruce's name to a woman. I didn't know this account existed.

I felt sick. I was shaking and my head was spinning.

A lot of money had been transferred to a woman I didn't know.

Could Bruce be the victim of a scam?

I called him immediately. "Bruce, can you tell me who this woman is that you are sending all this money to?"

"Are you checking on me? Did you hire a private detective or something?"

"No, Bruce. I just read this letter from the bank."

There was a long pause.

He told me that he would come home to explain everything.

At that point I still wanted to trust Bruce, I didn't want to think the worst. I assumed he had a good explanation for the money transfer.

When he came home we sat at the dining table.

He said, "The money was sent to help this woman's mother get an operation because they were very poor and need the money."

Later I found out the truth. The money went for a woman to get breast implants.

———————◆————————

Feeling the need to engage with other people and new ideas, I decided to go back to school. And what was the first class I signed up for? Eternal marriage, of course! I became obsessed with reading anything that could help save my marriage.

I had grown up hearing the phrase popularized by former President of The Church of Jesus Christ of Latter-day Saints, David O. McKay, "No other success can compensate the failure in the home."

I refused to become a failure. So, I grasped for anything that would keep my marriage from failing.

Every day I read or heard wonderful, positive quotes about marriage—it was like rubbing salt in my wounds.

Everything I was hearing in that class struck a deep chord in my soul. My marriage to Bruce had come to the point where the attributes of love, faith, repentance, respect, and loyalty were no longer present.

This is when I finally admitted that Bruce's love for me had died. This meant that our marriage was not eternal. The commitment was no longer there. He didn't want to grow old with me. His love was conditioned on me still looking young, thin and beautiful, which is a complete opposite of what true, eternal love is. This is when I knew I needed to find someone who would love me for who I was today and for who I would become tomorrow and decades after tomorrow, not for who I had been at age twenty-one.

By this time, I had a better understanding of who I was and what I had to offer a partner.

The suspense of waiting to hear what would happen to those boys in El Salvador ended up stretching over two months.

The agony I felt for my marriage would last longer after the judge signed the divorce decree because, and it may seem ridiculous, but I was still hoping for a miracle that Bruce would come back to me.

He never did.

And the angel said unto them,
Fear not: for, behold, I bring you good tidings
of great joy, which shall be to all people.
For unto us is born this day in the City of David
a Saviour which, is Christ the Lord.

— Luke 2:10–11

14

My Christmas Wish

*O*N DECEMBER 22, 2005, two days before Christmas Eve, I received a call from my mother. She was extremely excited. "The charges were dropped! The boys are free!"

What a big relief that was! Justice had been served, and the infamous "bondsmen" were finally free to go home.

I didn't pull off this minor miracle by myself. Yes, wearing my honorary consul hat in speaking face to face with their judge had a huge impact, but if it hadn't been for the efforts of my uncle, my sister, and my mother the outcome would have been very different. I also believe one of the reasons the young men were released was because so many people were praying for them.

For the young men and their families, their Christmas wish had come true. Eddy, Richard, and Thomas were home before Christmas. What a sweet reunion that must have been.

I admired how Eddy's family had resolved to let their anger go and in its place, they welcomed peace. I never once heard them complain about their son being detained in jail.

So why couldn't I do the same? I decided to find a way to let my bitterness and anger go, too. I wanted to find the same inner peace they had.

My struggle to free those young men had freed me, too. When I came back from El Salvador, I knew I was a person of value. I had done something that very few people can claim to have done. I had influenced a judge to soften her heart, and in doing so got three guys out of jail. I had seen the hand of the Lord guiding me, and I knew my prayers had been answered.

A miracle had taken place because some mortal *Ministering Angels,* had believed in me.

But, I had made a Christmas wish of my own— that Bruce would come to his senses and reclaim our marriage. At first I thought God had ignored my wish because it didn't' come true. My husband didn't return by Christmas despite the fact that I had put his name on the prayer roll every time I attended the temples of the Church of Jesus Christ of Latter-day Saints.

And yet, as I look back on that Christmas, I recognize that my wish—at least the most important part of it—was granted after all. This would be the first Christmas in twenty plus years that Bruce would not be part of the family's celebration, and I felt terribly alone!

My family seemed to see the distress I was in, and they rallied around me. My mother, my daughters, my sisters, and their families—all came to the frigid climate of Salt Lake City to spend the holidays with me. The warmth they brought with them filled my heart, and for a while my loneliness fled.

I didn't know it then, but that was a very special Christmas for our family. Since then, we haven't had a Christmas family reunion where we all came together.

PART TWO

Lessons Learned

These things have I spoken unto you,
that my joy might remain in you,
and that your joy might be full.

— JOHN 15:11

15

Life Is Designed for Joy

*T*HE MEN IN JAIL found a way to experience joy. They left their house every day to help the community. There were even rumors that one of them found a girlfriend. The people in the town knew them well enough to trust them. Although their lives were placed on hold those few months, they did the best they could with what they had.

For me, the way I found inner peace and joy was to focus on things other than my pending divorce. I learned to live without Bruce. I went back to school to finish my degree at Brigham Young University. I found many opportunities to help others, and I found happiness in doing those things I love. That time in my life that felt I was in limbo gave me the opportunity to learn new things, to travel, and to serve others.

They say that when it rains it pours, and for me this proved to be true. I also lost my father during the same time. But his passing proved to be a tender mercy because his inheritance money enabled me to survive those long years while the divorce was still up in the air.

In retrospect, I don't understand why I prolonged the agony for so long, other than I was waiting for a miracle. In my faith, we have the opportunity to receive priesthood blessings to help with, healing and other situations in our lives.

I had been given a blessing stating that my life would become wonderful again and everything would be restored. From that, I honestly thought Bruce would one day come back and be his old self again. I felt that waiting on him was what my mother calls "your cross."

At one time or another we all carry a burden or face a trial that challenges our strength and endurance. It may be an illness or a loss of some kind.

By coming to terms with my reality, I discovered

the secret to joy. Our current prophet of the Church of Jesus Christ of Latter-day Saints, President Russell M. Nelson explains.

"Life is filled with detours and dead ends, trials and challenges of every kind. Each of us has likely had times when distress, anguish, and despair almost consumed us. Yet we are here to have joy?

"Yes, the answer is a resounding yes!

"The joy we feel has little to do with the circumstances of our lives and everything to do with the focus of our lives.

"When the focus of our lives is on . . . Jesus Christ and His gospel, we can feel joy regardless of what is happening—or not happening—in our lives"

Be strong and courageous. Do not be afraid or terrified . . ., for the Lord your God goes with you; he will never leave you nor forsake you.

— DEUTERONOMY 31:6, NEW INTERNATIONAL VERSION

16

You Are Never Alone

$\mathcal{E}$ VEN IN MY DARKEST MOMENTS I was never alone, and neither were the bondsmen. They had their families and also me and my family praying for them. Luckily, we believed in them and got involved.

I have sometimes wondered if I had not been in the middle of a pending divorce and was experiencing a seemingly happy life, if I would have cared that much. It is one thing to have empathy; it is another to do something about it.

This time I acted—and I did all I could for them.

As I look back at those hard days, I am reminded of what former president of The Church of Jesus

Christ of Latter-day Saints, Thomas S. Monson said: "[God] will not always take your afflictions from you, but He will comfort and lead you with love through whatever storm you face" ("Looking Back and Moving Forward." *Liahona,* May 2008, 90).

My personal storm felt more like a hurricane at times. But now, as I look back, I find that a lot of good came out of what I thought, at the time was tragic.

On my fiftieth birthday, I received this note from my friend Jan:

> I am sure you never imagined all the twists and turns your life would take by your fiftieth birthday! We certainly never know what life is going to throw our way. But I must say that your best birthday gift must be the three wonderful young women that your beautiful girls have turned out to be. I admire them all, but it has been a special privilege to get to know Mindy as her young women leader. She is an exceptional young lady, and I think it is a testament to you as a mother that this sweet young girl has come through all the change in her life with such a mature attitude and willingness

to embrace new experiences in her life. We will certainly miss her at young women's. I hope your fiftieth year is a marvelous beginning to your new life's adventure.

She was so right! My daughters are all super awesome! And I had so many women around me who served as my girls' surrogate mothers, and I will forever be grateful to all of them.

Thinking of all those who have made a difference in my life, I was reminded of this quote:

"Some people move our souls to dance. They awaken us to a new understanding with the passing whisper of their wisdom. Some people make the sky more beautiful to gaze upon. They stay in our lives for awhile, leave footprints on our hearts, and we are never, ever the same." – FLAVIA WEEDN

In their hearts humans plan their course,
but the Lord establishes their steps.

PROVERBS 16:9, NEW INTERNATIONAL VERSION

17

Nothing Happens by Chance

OVER THE YEARS, I have learned as much by observing other people as I have in my own life. One thing is that nothing happens by chance.

There are no coincidences.

Eddy's mother found me through a mutual friend. It was not a stroke of luck that I had the support of three members of my family as well as the means to travel to El Salvador.

It was not an accident that I had an honorary consul card that allowed me to see the judge, and it was not pure chance that I happened to be in the positon to help.

Every day we are given opportunities to make a difference. Often, those opportunities come by way of spiritual promptings. We can choose to act on those promptings or choose not to. It takes courage to act on them, and it takes humility to accept the help someone else has been prompted to extend to us.

One day when we know we don't have much time left on this earth, we'll look back at our lives. It would be sad to find that we wish we had been happier, or more grateful, or more willing to smile and be kind to others. We probably are going to wish we had loved more and complained less. We might wish we had allowed ourselves to laugh out loud more often.

I can now reflect on the value of having had hard times. They've taught me lessons that I can now share with others to hopefully help them avoid those same pitfalls.

For anyone who is contemplating divorce, if you had children, there are still graduations, weddings, births of grandchildren, etc. that you both will be involved in.

You never divorce your children! I will give you my two cents: *Don't do it.* Unless you are experiencing brutal abuse, and if that is the case, then leave right away.

I learned that the only way to cope with challenging times was to forget about me and help others. I came to know that I had worth as a person and as a woman and that someone one day would appreciate me for who I was.

Fast forward, that day finally came. The man I am married to now is genuinely remarkable. He is not perfect, no one is; but he is a true gentleman. He is honest, faithful, an incredible father of eleven. He is an amazing, one-in-a-million type of a man, truly one of the finest to ever walk on this earth. That is not a cliché; it is the honest truth. I don't think meeting him was by chance either. It was meant to be.

My biggest concern at the time I remarried was my youngest daughter, Mindy. How would my new marriage affect her? But with a lot of prayer and counsel from loved ones, I learned that when you find the right person, why delay your happiness? Getting married to a wonderful man who has integrity and keeps his promises was exactly what I needed. And Mindy was nearly as happy and excited about it as I was.

Peace I leave with you, my peace I give unto you: not as the world giveth, give I unto you. Let not your heart be troubled, neither let it be afraid.

— JOHN 14:27

18

How to Obtain Peace

*T*HIS IS HOW IT HAPPENED. I was asked to
speak in church about forgiveness as it relates
to Christmas. As I was researching the topic, I
came across this counsel from former president of
The Church of Jesus Christ of Latter-day Saints,
Howard W. Hunter.

> *"This Christmas, mend a quarrel. Seek out
> a forgotten friend. Dismiss suspicion and
> replace it with trust . . . Keep a promise.
> Forgo a grudge. Forgive an enemy. Apologize.
> Try to understand . . . Think first of someone
> else. Be kind . . . Express your gratitude."*

Before I made the call, I was still feeling terribly hurt and unable to let go of those feelings. I was at one of the lowest points in my life. I could almost taste darkness, the bitterness, and the anger consuming my mind and soul, to the point of almost going insane. Yes, there is no question that I went a little insane. At the time, I was so focused on me as a victim and how I had been wronged that I couldn't connect fully with reality. All I wanted was to see the other person pay the consequences for hurting me and my family. I wanted the other person to get hurt just as badly as I had been, as if that would rectify the wrong done to me.

But life—at least a joyful, productive life—doesn't work that way. When we are in that kind of state, obsessed with ourselves and wallowing in self-pity, we miss out on all the good and wonderful things going on around us. It is human to focus on our hurts but trust me on this one because I have lived it. When you get so caught up in that mentality that you pretty much ignore everyone and everything else, you are ironically forgetting the most important person. YOU!

President Hunter's words gave me the strength I needed to tell my ex-husband that I forgave him. So, I called Bruce.

"I have no regrets. I have no hard feelings. I truly wish you a merry Christmas, and I hope the best for you. God Bless."

I will always remember that moment. For the first time in a long time, I felt peace. I was healed! I had learned that if you are willing to forgive, the Savior will gift you with internal peace, and trough the healing that accompanies that peace, you can move on.

My Christmas wish had come true!

He said, "I am sorry for all the pain I caused you. I hope you forgive me."

That was the very first time I had heard him say, "I'm sorry." It would have been fine if he hadn't said anything but his request for forgiveness was a bonus.

Let all bitterness, and wrath, and anger,
and clamour, and evil speaking, be put away from
you, with all malice: and be kind one to another,
tenderhearted, forgiving one another, even as
God for Christ's sake hath forgiven you.

– EPHESIANS 4:31–32

19

Let It Go

*T*HIS CHAPTER actually continues the theme introduced in the previous one, as it relates to the importance of forgiveness as a way of letting the hurt go. Forgiving and seeking forgiveness are so fundamentally important that I want to emphasize them.

You need to keep your sanity. You've no doubt heard the clever phrase: "Refusing to forgive is like taking poison and hoping the other person will die." The truth is, humans are imperfect. People are going to make mistakes and disappoint you. People are going to hurt you. All of us have been betrayed at one time or another—some in major ways, some in smaller ways. The most painful hurts come from those we love. But then, we have disappointed and hurt other people ourselves, especially those we care about. It is part of being human.

So what do we do when someone hurts us? We could hold onto the hurt and become resentful and bitter. Or we could forgive and move on. It is up to us. But from my own experience, it's better to do the latter. Hatred always fails, and bitterness always destroys. "Remember, heaven is filled with those who have this in common. They are forgiven. And they forgive" (Dieter F. Uchdorf, "The Merciful Obtain Mercy," *Ensign,* May 2012, 77).

I became both happier and stronger as soon as I was able to forgive and let go. I also felt at peace, and having that within oneself is an enormous blessing. The world may be filled with troubles and fears, but there is a center of peace in my soul that the world cannot touch. I know where I want to live for all eternity and with whom. Therefore, I need to have a firm conviction that nothing, including painful experiences, will stop me.

If you've ever made a Christmas wish and thought that it didn't come true, think again. It probably did. The Lord knows what is best for you, just as He knew what was best for me. He knew that in a few years, if I had hope and faith, I would marry an exceptionally wonderful man who appreciates me and treats me like his queen. We face the happy prospect of spending the rest of all our Christmases together.

My wish for you is that you focus on something other than your burdens and place your trust in the Lord's timing. Letting go of past hurts will make that possible.

For God so loved the world, that he gave his only begotten Son, that whosoever believeth in him should not perish, but have everlasting life.

– JOHN: 3:16

20

How a
Jail Cell Saved Christmas

SO HOW DID A JAIL CELL save my Christmas? You've probably already figured it out. It was when I forgot about myself and began to care for those three young men incarcerated in El Salvador.

For the first time, my celebration of the season had a real meaning. All the anger and sorrow I was feeling about being betrayed dissolved when I turned my inward thoughts outward to the needs of others. As a result, I was able to enjoy Christmas in a way I never had before.

A bonus was finding out that there is life after divorce. With time, I finally healed. In fact, I became a better person by dealing with a broken heart. I went through a refiner's fire and discovered power in the atonement of Jesus Christ. Before this trial, I never gave much thought to what Christ's atoning sacrifice meant in my life. But my anguish forced me to rely on Him, to seek healing and to gain the power to hope again. His gift to me was a renewal of life.

And this is His perfect gift to everyone. I am sure Eddy, Richard and Thomas, felt that renewal. Their incarceration didn't define them. No matter what people said about the "bondsmen" they knew inside who they were. They had the Savior's assurance that they were innocent, and that gave them peace.

So, this is the answer for all who seek to save Christmas for themselves. All they need to do is find others in need and help them. Doing so honors Jesus and serves as the perfect way of giving thanks for His perfect gift of everlasting life. This is the gift only He can give, and it is the reason why we celebrate Christmas.

Over six decades of my life, I have come to see Christmas with new eyes. I am old enough to remember many Christmases. They have all been glorious. But I have learned that it isn't the presents that make them great. I've learned that Christmas, at its best, is a celebration of the gospel of Jesus Christ, which can bring us joy and peace in every situation. As we follow the example of Jesus and do what He has taught us to do, love our neighbor, we are blessed with the influence of the Holy Ghost. Then, during times of trouble or fear, the Spirit will be with us, filling our hearts with peace.

Elder D. Todd Christofferson explained:

> *"People want to know if they can have hope. I say to all of us, the answer is yes. With faith in the merciful Redeemer and His power, potential despair turns to hope. . . My hope is that when the tide of disappointment and misfortune turns toward us—and from time to time it surely will—that we will remember that when we look toward the Lord in faith, He will guide us through life's difficulties— whatever they may be."*

(facebook.com/lds.d.todd.christofferson.posts,1314673525288726)

I will leave you with some final advice. Doing these three things has brought the most peace into my life. I believe they will do the same for you. Never in my life have I felt so strongly a responsibility to share these ideas.

Pray

Think of Father in Heaven daily. Start your day kneeling in sincere prayer, thanking Him for a new day and asking for His help on anything you need to accomplish. He will comfort and sustain you. He will help you do more and be more than you can ever do or become on your own. At the end of your day, before you retire to bed, thank Him for the blessings he bestowed upon you that day. Having a thankful heart, no matter the circumstances, will help you feel peace. I usually write in my journal the things I am thankful for each day.

Read the Scriptures and Inspired Messages

The divine messages found in the scriptures are there for us to contemplate and apply. Reading the scriptures daily is one of the greatest sources of strength in my life.

Another source of inspiration is pondering on the talks from The Church of Jesus Christ of

Latter-day Saints general conference. These are broadcast every April and October throughout the world. General conference includes ten hours of inspirational, uplifting, life-changing messages from incredible speakers. The talks are given on a myriad of topics by men and women who have been anointed and called to serve Jesus Christ. The topics may include faith, hope, happiness, charity, marriage, family relationships, emergency preparedness, making wise choices, divine nature, self-improvement, and dealing with adversities.

I never, ever miss general conference! I always listen to the talks as they are being given live and then go back later to read them and re-listen when I need direction or comfort on one of the topics addressed. The talks given in past conferences have gotten me through all my hard times and have given me hope. They have inspired me to continually work to be a better person. They have helped me make better decisions. They have brightened my path when the way ahead was dark and unclear. Above all, they have given me tremendous strength and peace.

Celebrate Christmas in a Meaningful Way

I learned this secret from my mother. Each December she worked hard putting together baskets of food to give away. In El Salvador, you don't have to look too hard to find people who are suffering from hunger.

I don't necessarily mean for you to do the same. Just make sure that each Christmas reflects the Savior's love. Perhaps that means simply making a special effort to count your blessings.

I love this quote:

"Our celebration of Christmas should be a reflection of the love and selflessness taught by the Savior. Giving, not getting, brings to full bloom the Christmas spirit. We feel more kindly one to another. We reach out in love to help those less fortunate. Our hearts are softened. Enemies forgiven, friends remembered, and God obeyed. The spirit of Christmas illuminates the picture window of the soul, and we look out upon the world's busy life and become more interested in people than in things."

– Thomas S. Monson

In summary, doing those simple things is how I celebrate Christmas every day of the year. Think of all the Savior has done for you over the past year, and then do something special for someone else in remembrance of His gifts to you. The great gift of His atonement will work in every aspect of your life the way it has worked in mine if you only let Him into your heart. He's already given you His Christmas Gift—a gift that is perfect in every way. Now it is up to you to receive it, and when you do, your life will never be the same!

The End

Epilogue

This book took me almost twenty years of hard experiences to write. I hope that after having read it, you consider me your friend, someone you can trust. At least trust the life lessons I've shared. They are part of an important legacy I want to leave behind when my life is over. I want to be remembered as someone who did her very best to do good in the world. That's important to me.

I don't know what it is with me anymore, but I don't care about money, prestige, or possessions the way I did when I was younger. As the Spanish saying goes, *Estoy más cerca del arpa celestial que de la guitarra*—I am closer to the celestial harp than to the guitar.

What I care about today is helping others. Yes, I do. I care about you! I hope I have been able to show you how I found peace and joy at one of the darkest times in my life, a time when I felt scared, sad, lonely and angry. I wanted to give people like me—and possibly you—some hope. I wanted others to learn to be in tune with the Spirit and to accept the ministering of angels, who are providing us with incredible tender mercies if we let them.

If your life is fabulous and going the way you want it, congratulations! However, be prepared, we all at some point in our lives get our hearts broken. If you are experiencing a broken heart at this moment, I hope you learned from my experience that if you want to heal, you need to focus on something other than what you are going through. This is easier said than done, but I promise you, your agony won't last forever. I am proof of that. As former President of The church of Jesus Christ of Latter-day Saints, Gordon B. Hinckley often said, "In the end, everything will work out."

Special Thanks

I WAS INVITED to a retreat at the Timepiece Ranch, owned by Richard Paul Evans. I knew who Mr. Evans was even before he wrote his first book, *The Christmas Box,* which has sold millions of copies. I have always wondered, how did he do it? How did he self-publish his first book? Very few people have accomplished what he has done as an author, writing and publishing not just one book but dozens of best sellers.

One of the reasons he does so well is that he tells stories that touch your heart. I first read *The Christmas Box* over thirty years ago. I had just lost a baby sister, and the book touched me deeply. It spoke to the heart of my mother, as well, as it has to the hearts of many other women who have lost a child. For any mother, the book is achingly poignant.

Like the story in *The Christmas Box,* I have also experienced loss. Mine was not the loss of a child, however, but the loss of my marriage being torn apart. *How a Jail Cell Saved Christmas* is about the trauma of that loss—and how I healed from it.

I kept wishing to someday write about it, but never got motivated to start.

That changed when I received an invitation to attend a writing workshop at Timepiece Ranch. During my time there, I came to feel that I could do it. Each day people would read for five minutes to receive feedback from the group. The fact that you get to rub shoulders with accomplished authors who are willing to give you a hand builds confidence and encourages persistence.

I highly recommend Author Ready to any aspiring author. There isn't a more hands-on supportive community out there. If you want to write a book, working with Richard Paul Evans and his team at Author Ready is the smartest way to do it. Thank you for being so talented with the written word, but more importantly for giving me this opportunity. Thank you for sharing your expertise with me. Your passion for writing makes me want to work harder every day. To everyone in the Author Ready community; I am grateful to you for your support and for being people I can depend on.

A Sneak Peek Into My Next Book

Title to be determined — Releasing in 2026

I REMEMBER VIVIDLY the moment I decided to immigrate to the United States. It was when a government coup took place initiating a civil war in El Salvador. My parents and I were in our car going along a street downtown San Salvador. I was looking at all the holes on the walls made by bullets, when we came to a stop. I looked out the window and saw an automatic weapon pointing at me.

The gun barrel was right between my eyes. The possibility of dying at that precise moment was real to me.

I immediately went to see my boyfriend David, and begged him to move away. "Please, get out of here. Don't you see, you could get killed!"

He held me tight and softly whispered in my ear, "I can't. I need to stay where I am needed the most." Those were the last words I heard from him. Shortly after, I was attending my boyfriend's funeral.

About the Author

VERONICA R. DE ALMEIDA was first published in 2016 when a chapter she wrote was featured in the book *In the Spirit of Jershon*. Since that time, she has developed a love for writing. In addition to sitting on several boards, she is actively involved in managing her own real estate rental business.

Veronica is a native of El Salvador and a former teacher. She was appointed Honorary Consul of El Salvador to Utah in 2001. Her interests include Latin American studies, politics, religion, reading, writing, family history, and spending time with her grandchildren. Veronica and her husband blended two families making them the parents of eleven children and twenty-eight grandchildren.

Recently they have served in several international and domestic areas on assignment from The Church of Jesus Christ of Latter-day Saints, including the Caribbean, the Philippines, South America, the United States and Canada. She currently resides in Utah.

For more information, or to connect with the author, please visit: **veronicardealmeida.com**.

The candle represents the light of Christ.